Voices From The Past ★ ★ ★ ★ ★ ★ ★ ★ ★ ★

WORLD WAR I

KATHLYN GAY   MARTIN GAY

Twenty-First Century Books
A Division of Henry Holt and Company
New York

Twenty-First Century Books
A Division of Henry Holt and Company, Inc.
115 West 18th Street
New York, NY 10011

Henry Holt® and colophon are trademarks of
Henry Holt and Company, Inc.
Publishers since 1866

Published in Canada by Fitzhenry & Whiteside Ltd.
195 Allstate Parkway, Markham, Ontario L3R 4T8

Library of Congress Cataloging-in-Publication Data
Gay, Kathlyn.
World War I / Kathlyn Gay and Martin Gay. — 1st ed.
p. cm. — (Voices from the past)
Includes bibliographical references and index.
1. World War, 1914–1918—Juvenile literature. [1. World War, 1914–1918.] I. Gay,
Martin, 1950– . II. Title. III. Series: Gay, Kathlyn. Voices from the past.
D522.7.G38 1995   95–12300
940.3—dc20   CIP
                                                                 AC

ISBN 0–8050–2848–X
First Edition 1995

Printed in the United States of America
All first editions are printed on acid-free paper ∞.
10 9 8 7 6 5 4 3 2 1

Maps by Vantage Art, Inc.
Cover design by Karen Quigley
Interior design by Kelly Soong

Cover: *Men of Iron* by Don Troiani
Courtesy of Historical Art Prints, Southbury, Connecticut

Photo credits

pp. 11, 25, 57: Brown Brothers; pp. 12, 23: UPI/Bettmann; pp. 13, 18, 34, 46, 50, 52:
The Bettmann Archive; p. 20: New York Times/NYT Pictures; p. 29: U.S. Army
Signal Corps; p. 38: *The Rock of the Marne* by Charles H. McBarron, courtesy of the
U.S. Army Center of Military History; p. 40: Dept. of the Army, National Guard
Bureau, Washington, D.C.; p. 43: AP/Wide World Photos; p. 53: Sophia Smith
Collection, Smith College; p. 54: FPG International.

Contents

Acknowledgments

Some of the research for this series depended upon the special efforts of Dean Hamilton, who spent many hours locating primary source materials and other references on America's wars and sorting out appropriate stories among the many personal accounts available. Especially helpful was his work at the archival library of the University of South Florida at Tampa, researching for Spanish-American War and Civil War narratives. For the *World War I* title in this series, Dean also applied his special talents interviewing several of the few remaining veterans of WW I, obtaining their highly personal recollections, which the veterans allowed us to include. Thanks, Dean.

In addition, we would like to thank Lt. Col. (retired) John McGarrahan for locating narratives about personal experiences in the War of 1812, available in the archives at the Lilly Library, Indiana University, Bloomington, Indiana. We also thank Douglas Gay for obtaining narratives on the battle of Tippecanoe at the Tippecanoe County Historical Association in Lafayette, Indiana. Portions of these accounts are included in the *War of 1812* title in this series.

—*Kathlyn Gay and Martin Gay*

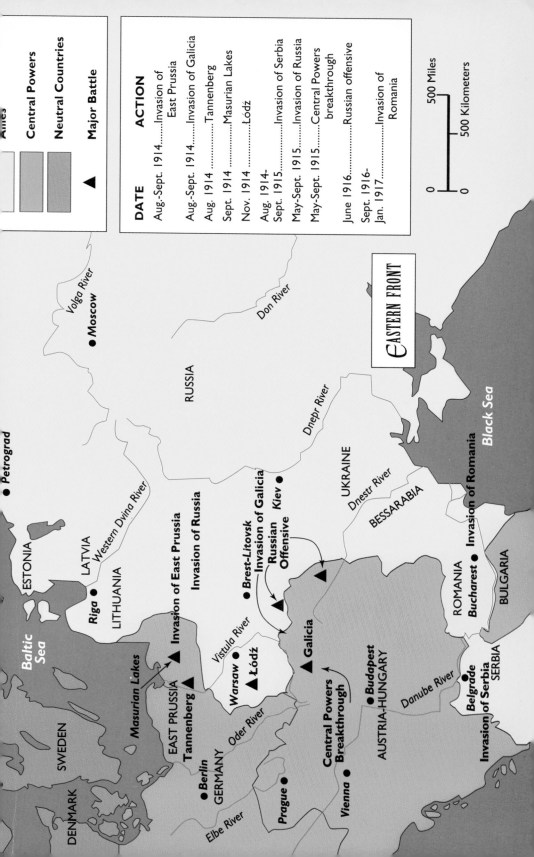

EASTERN FRONT

DATE	ACTION
Aug.-Sept. 1914	Invasion of East Prussia
Aug.-Sept. 1914	Invasion of Galicia
Aug. 1914	Tannenberg
Sept. 1914	Masurian Lakes
Nov. 1914	Łódź
Aug. 1914-Sept. 1915	Invasion of Serbia
May-Sept. 1915	Invasion of Russia
May-Sept. 1915	Central Powers breakthrough
June 1916	Russian offensive
Sept. 1916-Jan. 1917	Invasion of Romania

Allies
Central Powers
Neutral Countries

▲ Major Battle

0   500 Miles

0   500 Kilometers

DENMARK

SWEDEN

Baltic Sea

Petrograd

ESTONIA

LATVIA

Riga

LITHUANIA

Western Dvina River

Moscow

Volga River

RUSSIA

Don River

Dnepr River

Invasion of East Prussia
Invasion of Russia

Masurian Lakes

EAST PRUSSIA

Tannenberg

GERMANY

Berlin

Vistula River

Warsaw

Łódź

Oder River

Prague

Brest-Litovsk
Invasion of Galicia
Russian Offensive

Kiev

UKRAINE

Dnestr River

BESSARABIA

Galicia

Central Powers Breakthrough

Budapest

AUSTRIA-HUNGARY

Vienna

Elbe River

Danube River

Belgrade

Invasion of Serbia

SERBIA

ROMANIA

Bucharest

Invasion of Romania

BULGARIA

Black Sea

WESTERN AND ITALIAN FRONTS

Date	Action
Aug. 4, 1914	Start of invasion of Belgium and France
Sept. 6-9, 1914	First Battle of the Marne
Oct.-Nov. 1914 & Apr. 1915-June 1915	Battles of Ypres
Sept. 1917	Eleven Battles of the Isonzo
Feb.-July 1916	Verdun
May 1916	Asiago offensive
May 1916	Trentino offensive
May 31-June 1, 1916	Battle of Jutland (naval)
July 1-Nov. 1916	Battle of the Somme
Apr. 1917	Vimy Ridge
July-Nov. 1917	Passchendaele
Oct. 1917	Caporetto
Mar. 21, 1918	St.-Quentin
Apr. 1918	Lys River offensive
May 1918	Château-Thierry
May 1918	Cantigny
May-June 1918	Aisne offensive
June 1918	Belleau Wood
June 1918	Piave River
July-Aug. 1918	Second Battle of the Marne
Sept. 1918	St.-Mihiel
Sept.-Nov. 1918	Meuse-Argonne offensive
Oct. 1918	Vittorio Veneto
Nov. 3, 1918	Trieste seized

Legend:
- Allies
- Central Powers
- Neutral countries
- ▲ Major Battle

Map labels:

GREAT BRITAIN

North Sea

English Channel

Le Havre

Calais

Battle of Ypres

Passchendaele

Lys River Offensive

Lys R.

Vimy Ridge

Somme R.

Battle of the Somme

Cantigny

NETHERLANDS

BELGIUM

Belleau Wood

Aisne Offensive

Aisne R.

Château-Thierry

Verdun

Meuse-Argonne Offensive

St.-Mihiel

LUXEMBOURG

Moselle River

Rhine River

GERMANY

Second Battle of the Marne

Paris

Marne River

Seine River

First Battle of the Marne

Troyes

Orleans

Loire River

FRANCE

SWITZERLAND

AUSTRIA-HUNGARY

Trento

Trentino Offensive

Asiago Offensive

Verona

Adige River

Venice

Lake Garda

Po River

ITALY

Piave R.

Vittorio Veneto

Piave River

Eleven Battles of the Isonzo

Caporetto

Trieste

ISTRIA

Rijeka

North Sea

NORWAY

SWEDEN

DENMARK

Battle of Jutland

GREAT BRITAIN

0   50   100 Miles

One

★

THE GREAT WAR

"I was so glad it was over. I got tired of looking at the dead troops. It was awful."[1] That's how ninety-three-year-old Lawrence Dorsey summed up his World War I experiences as a gunner on the USS *South Dakota.* He was seventeen years old in 1917 when he was assigned to the *Dakota,* which escorted U.S. troopships to France, where fierce fighting took place; the ship then returned with American casualties. On November 11, 1993, Dorsey, along with thousands of other veterans, celebrated the seventy-fifth anniversary of the armistice that ended what was then called the Great War.

An estimated 35,000 to 60,000 World War I veterans are still living (many are over one hundred years of age). In interviews granted during the armistice anniversary week, their comments were similar to Dorsey's. They protested the "senseless killings." Yet in their youth, the enlistees were eager to get to Europe. "We all wanted to learn to shoot guns. I wanted to learn to shoot a cannon," explained ninety-five-year-old George Harris of New Orleans. "We were going to . . . make the world safe for democracy."[2]

Long before the U.S. military forces were sent to fight in World War I, there was political unrest across much of Europe because of nationalistic pride and the belief that loyalty to one's nation was more important than any other cause. Individual nations wanted to acquire more territory and military power. To justify a buildup of arms, national governments encouraged separateness and divisiveness. People in one nation disliked and often hated people of other nations who did not share their religion or way of life.

In western Europe, Germany and France fought over territory, and Germany became the most powerful European commercial and industrial country. Great Britain, an island nation, created a powerful navy to protect its shores, but Germany challenged the British strength with a buildup of its naval fleet.

On the eastern side, Russia was weakened by internal political intrigue and revolutionary rumblings. Yet this did not stop Russians from trying to gain land that was controlled by the alliance of Austria-Hungary. Others also coveted land under Austrian and Hungarian rule. The small neighboring kingdom of Serbia hoped to gain the southern province in the Balkans known as Bosnia and Herzegovina, where many people of Serbian ancestry lived. Italy wanted to take over lands where Italians had settled but which belonged to Austria. In addition, people of various national ancestries living in territory ruled by Austria-Hungary sought their freedom.

THE SPARK OF WAR

The conflicting national interests in western and eastern Europe drove the major countries to form protective coalitions, even with nations that had once been bitter enemies. Smaller countries were forced to choose sides, and by 1914 Europe was separated into two heavily armed camps. Any spark would have been enough to ignite the war that everyone expected.

That spark was touched off in Sarajevo, the capital city

of Bosnia and Herzegovina (now the capital of Bosnia), where fighting over old land disputes has erupted again in recent times and continues to this day. In an attempt to ease tensions between Austria-Hungary and people in the Balkans, the Austrian archduke Francis Ferdinand and his wife, Sophie, made a ceremonial trip to Sarajevo.

Ferdinand was in line to be the next emperor of the Austro-Hungarian Empire. The archduke had made enemies in the neighboring kingdom of Serbia because he once favored the reorganization of the empire to create a third kingdom of Croatia. At the same time, Serbia was attempting to expand its power by bringing all of the ethnic Serbs—people who shared a similar way of life and language—under its dominion, so it had designs on Croatian territory as well.

As Ferdinand's caravan of open cars made its way through Sarajevo, it was attacked by a group of bomb-throwing terrorists who hoped to assassinate Ferdinand. Their grenade missed the archduke but killed others in the caravan. Terrified, the archduke's driver tried to escape by turning the carriage around and racing to the train depot. In an ironic twist of fate, he got lost and entered a street where nineteen-year-old Gavrilo Princip, a young Serbian nationalist, was hiding.

Princip was part of the terrorist group and he quickly realized a second opportunity to kill the archduke was at hand. He pulled out a pistol and began to fire, hitting Sophie, who had tried to shield her husband. Princip continued to fire and killed the archduke.

Rulers of Austria-Hungary believed the Serbian government had planned the attack, and they immediately invaded Serbia. This aggressive action prompted a full-scale war that eventually spread throughout Europe, to parts of the Middle East, and to areas of Africa and Asia where some European nations had established colonies.

This "war to end all wars," as many thought it would be, started on June 29, 1914, with the Austrian bombardment of Belgrade, the capital city of Serbia. Austrians relied on the fact that their ally Germany would jump into the fray should they themselves be attacked. They also were confident of acquiring land in Serbia.

However, the Russians came to the defense of the Serbs, with whom they shared a common ethnic ancestry, and the Germans then declared war on the Russians. The British and the French were obliged to defend the Russians because of a former alliance. Britain, France, Russia, Serbia, and numerous other nations, including Italy, which at first remained neutral, became known as the Associated Powers, or the Allies.

The German coalition with Austria-Hungary occupied the central section of Europe, and they became known as the Central Powers. They fought the Russians on the eastern front, hoping to contain them and then attack France. On the western front, the Germans aggressively invaded neutral Belgium in an attempt to surprise France with a quick occupying force. In the Battle of Liege, a stubborn Belgian force held up the advancing German army long enough to allow the French to mobilize men and arms to defend their border with Germany. In September, the French and British held off the Germans at the Marne River in what became known as the First Battle of the Marne.

When England declared war on Germany in August 1914, Canada immediately began to mobilize to aid the British war effort and in October sent 33,000 troops to Europe. Other divisions soon followed, and great numbers did not return—at least 55,000 Canadian soldiers died in the war.

Immense armies in Europe went into the field to fight

*Equipment on horse-drawn carts followed mounted troops
when the Germans invaded Belgium on August 4, 1914.*

with a vengeance and brutality that up to that time had never before been demonstrated. In a particularly devastating battle, the British Expeditionary Force, which included Canadian troops, was almost destroyed as the soldiers stopped a German advance at the bloody First Battle of Ypres in Belgium.

In October 1914, Turkey attacked Russia, bombarding ports on the Black Sea and sending in invasion forces. As a result, the Allies declared war on the Ottoman Empire (of which Turkey was a part). Turkey then laid mines in the Dardanelles, a strait between the Gallipoli Peninsula and the Turkish coast. This cut off all supply routes to Russia, so in January 1915, Russia asked the Allies for help. British, French, and some Australian and New Zealand troops were sent to open up the strait.

Ypres in Belgium was almost totally destroyed in World War I.

After destroying forts at the entrance of the strait, the Allies landed troops on Gallipoli, hoping Allied soldiers could push inland and secure the only available road for transporting supplies. But progress was slow, and in April the Central Powers were able to force the Allies to retreat, with an immense loss of lives on both sides. By the end of the year, the Allies began to evacuate the peninsula. They had accomplished nothing, and many historians have called the expedition a terrible waste.

NEW TYPES OF WARFARE

By the end of 1914, the war on the western front had settled into a stagnant but dangerous phase. From the North Sea to the Swiss border, each side dug a system of long, snakelike trenches protected by barbed wire and a machine gun. The first trench in each network was the firing line, then a cover trench was behind, followed by support, reserve, and communication trenches. Should the enemy break through the first line at any point, they could be hit with heavy artillery and fire from the next line. On each side, soldiers fired out across an expanse of land called no man's land, which separated the two sides.

A war of attrition was waged until the end of 1918. Each side tried to wear down the defenses of the other. Tactics and technology that were new to the battlefield were developed. The Germans used blimplike rigid airships called zeppelins, named for the ship's designer, Graf von Zeppelin, to spy on Allied positions and occasionally to drop bombs. Airplanes also were designed for warfare. After their speed and maneuverability were improved, the planes were used in midair battles known as dogfights.

The armored vehicle—the tank—also was improved and refined. Electronic communications in the form of the telephone and the wireless radio became common as the war progressed.

One of the most frightening advances in war technology was the development of poison gas. An anonymous soldier

Rigid airships called zeppelins were used by Germany in air raids against Great Britain.

who spent his time in the trenches as part of the British Expeditionary Force described this weaponry:

> Gas? What do you know of it, you people who have never heard earth and heaven rock with the frantic turmoil of the ceaseless bombardment? A crawling yellow cloud that pours in upon you, that gets you by the throat and shakes you as a huge mastiff might shake a kitten, leaves you burning in every nerve and vein of your body with pain unthinkable; your eyes starting from their sockets; your face turned yellow-green.[3]

Eventually countermeasures were developed to deal with the gas attacks, but misery and death were constant companions, as the unknown soldier pointed out:

> Stench? Did you ever breathe air foul with the gases arising from a thousand rotting corpses? Dirt? Have you ever fought half madly thru days and nights and weeks unwashed, with feverish rests between long hours of agony, while the guns boom their awful symphony of death, and the bullets zip-zip-zip ceaselessly along the trench edge that is your sky-line—and your death line too, if you stretch and stand up?[4]

AMERICAN CONCERNS

Even though the United States had not declared war in 1915, some Americans who were in Europe at the time supported the military efforts of the French and British. One was a young woman who joined the French Red Cross and was known only as Mademoiselle Miss. Her correspondence to a friend in the States described the scenes around the army hospital near the great battlefields of the Marne, where she was stationed:

October 8, 1915

> You know how it is in the trenches,—load and fire most of the time. That's how it is here. During the last week, we have averaged 25 operations daily. One day we had 33.... But the struggle, and the sense that one is saving bits from the wreckage, doesn't give one a chance to be mastered by the unutterable woe....
>
> I haven't the time nor the heart to tell you the tale of my days, but I shall never get hardened to last agonies and heart-broken families. And when my little No. 23 flung out his arms last night to say "Good-by" (he knew he was going)—"O my sister, my sister! kiss me!"—I tell you it took control to finish giving the last of my 34 anti-tetanus injections a few minutes later.
>
> Speaking of injections,—*please* send me some platinum needles, big and little. I hope you will send cotton and gauze soon, and rubber gloves.[5]

Few Americans were as involved as Mademoiselle Miss in the early war efforts, but the majority of the population in the United States sympathized with the Allies. Officially the United States remained neutral, and Americans generally supported President Woodrow Wilson, a brilliant scholar who was deathly afraid that this conflict would change the face of the earth.

Wilson did all he could to "keep us out of war," as his campaign slogan attested. The Germans, however, used yet another technical advance in warfare—the submarine—to finally prompt the United States to break out of its isolation.

Two

★

U.S. PREPARATIONS FOR WAR

On May 7, 1915, a German submarine surprised the British passenger liner *Lusitania*. A torpedo struck the unarmed ship and it sank to the bottom of the ocean, off the coast of Ireland. Hundreds of men, women, and children lost their lives. One hundred twenty-nine were Americans, and citizens in the United States were outraged by what they considered an immoral and cowardly act of war against neutral noncombatants.

The German government had established a war zone around the British Isles in an effort to negate the considerable strength of the English navy. One primary means of patrolling this area was with submersible craft known as U-boats. First used by Americans in the Revolutionary and Civil Wars, the submarine was modified by the Germans to become an effective war machine.

The submarine's greatest advantage was the element of surprise. After spotting a ship, a crew could fire a torpedo from under the surface, virtually guaranteeing no detection. The German government warned all neutral countries of their intent to utilize that advantage by sinking any ship discovered in the war zone.

The United States government protested mightily before and after the attack on the *Lusitania*. President

Wilson argued that submarine warfare violated the "principles of justice and humanity." The submarine could not warn a ship of its presence without being vulnerable to a counterattack, and because of its size, it could not take prisoners or rescue survivors. Although the Germans would not admit to acting illegally, by 1916 they had apologized and paid some money to the survivors and families affected by the sinking of the *Lusitania*.

President Wilson warned that he would not guarantee U.S. neutrality if the German government continued to declare unrestricted warfare and blockade the British with submarines. The Germans agreed not to attack as long as the British would not violate international law. Most Americans were happy that their president had avoided war with an honorable solution.

THE FINAL OUTRAGE

Wilson was encouraged by news in December of 1916 that Germany's ministers were ready to negotiate a peace. But the Germans were only buying a little more time—keeping the United States out of the conflict so they could launch an all-out attack on French and British positions. Success against the Russians on the eastern front had bolstered German expectations for a swift victory, and in January 1917 they announced some very harsh terms for peace. Once again, they began to attack any ship they spotted.

On March 18, 1917, U-boats sank several American cargo ships, forcing President Wilson to face the grim facts. He could not ignore the willful violations of the neutrality of his country, and the English and French could not hold out against the Germans unless they received reinforcements.

At first, Wilson had hoped that money and matériel would be adequate to bolster the Allied defenses, but

A German U-boat sinks an American freighter.

England and France made it clear that troops were needed in very short order. On April 2, Wilson addressed a special session of Congress. "The world must be made safe for democracy," he said. As he prepared to ask Congress for a declaration of war, he noted:

> It is a fearful thing to lead this great peaceful people into war, into the most disastrous of all wars, civilization itself seeming to be in the balance. But the right is more precious than peace, and we shall fight for the things which we have always carried nearest our hearts ... for democracy, for the right of those who submit to authority to have a voice in their own governments, for the rights and liberties of small nations, for a universal dominion of right by such a concert of free peoples as shall bring peace and safety to all nations and make the world at last free.[1]

THE DRAFT

At the time Congress declared war, the United States was barely prepared to defend its own borders. The nation, which had relied on a citizen volunteer army, had to adopt conscription, or a military draft. The Selective Service Act was quickly passed, in spite of highly vocal opposition by those who felt such a law was in itself a threat to democracy.

Emma Goldman, a radical political activist of the day, made speeches throughout the land protesting involuntary military service. She also organized the No-Conscription League in New York, which was so successful that within two weeks at least 8,000 people promised not to register for the draft. Goldman was fearless in her denunciation of government actions that she felt trampled on the rights of the individual. In one fervent speech, she declared:

> We, who came from Europe, came here looking to America as the promised land. I came believing that liberty was a fact. And when we today resent war and conscription, it is not that we are foreigners and don't care, it is precisely because we love America and we are opposed to war.[2]

Although thousands protested the draft, there was not nationwide support for Goldman's thinking. Nevertheless, the government did not want to take chances with demonstrators like Goldman. Authorities called her the "most dangerous woman in America"—which was never proven—and arrested her. She was charged with breaking a new law that made her antidraft activities a conspiracy against the federal government. Goldman was convicted, served two years in a federal prison, and was deported to Russia in 1919.

As the United States continued to prepare for war in 1917, the U.S. Navy, which was comprised of about 800,000

Emma Goldman came to the United States from Russia in 1885. She spoke frequently against the draft in World War I.

sailors at that time, quickly deployed crews aboard ships to lay mines in the North Sea. U.S. Navy ships also acted as protective convoys for British ships threatened by German U-boats.

From a regular army of some 128,000, eventually five million U.S. men and women were put into service. Although, as in previous wars, blacks were discriminated against and segregated in both military and private life, Americans of African descent eventually made up more than one-third of the U.S. forces sent to Europe. Several all-black regiments saw combat, but most African-American soldiers were assigned to service battalions.

VOLUNTEERS

By the summer of 1917, nine million Americans had registered for the draft, but only a portion of the draftees were needed—many other Americans volunteered for the armed forces. Norbert Hayden was typical of those who felt it was their duty to join up and do their part. Born in 1896 in Missouri, Hayden went to enlist in the spring of 1918, when he was twenty-one. As he recalled:

> I went down to St. Louis to the recruiting office to volunteer for the navy. All the navy at that time was volunteer. The recruiting officer was standing outside in uniform, and he had a scale there to weigh you with before he let you in. He weighed me and told me I was two or three pounds short. He told me if I put the additional weight on I might be successful. He told me maybe it would be a good idea to eat a lot of bananas, said they would put some weight on you quick.

Hayden took the advice and a week later returned to the recruitment office. He was almost accepted but, as he reported, "they detected a varicose vein," a swollen vein in his leg, and he "couldn't pass on that." So the following day, Hayden went to the St. Louis City Hospital for surgery to remove the vein. When his leg finally healed, Hayden "went back to the recruiting office . . . and everything went through good."[3]

Hayden could have gone home twice, confident that he had tried to do his duty. But, he stated flatly, "I wasn't yellow." Still, he had to go through even one more trial before he could get into the real action. Along with thousands of other recruits, he was assigned to boot camp—basic training—at the Great Lakes Naval Base in northern Illinois, where his brother was also sent. While he was there, the camp was hit with a deadly influenza outbreak that took many lives. As he explained: ·

> I did hear them say that an express car load of bodies went out of the [base] hospital every day . . . and I was scared to

death that my brother was in there too. He was in a different barracks up there and we were quarantined. I didn't
know if he was sick. They was detailing different bunches to
go up to the hospital to help embalm them, and I was always
afraid I'd run into my brother up there.... Wouldn't that be
terrible? He was sick but he lived.[4]

Hayden eventually made it to New York City, where he
was assigned to duty on one of several large transports, each
carrying 8,000 men to France. The movement of troops and
arms was an immense task, and many Americans were
involved in the effort. At the same time, the military began to
welcome women into the service.

"Having women [in the military] was an innovation.
And they started from scratch," related Claire Powers, who
joined the navy in 1918. Instead of going back to college that
summer in Salem, Massachusetts, she went to live near her
mother in Elliot, Maine, "near the Navy yard," she explained.
"I saw all these girls in their pretty uniforms going by every
day, and it took me all summer long to make up my mind not
to go back to school but instead to enlist. Navy girls were
everywhere and Navy men were everywhere. I was twenty
years old then."

Powers worked in the summer to put herself through
school, but everyone talked about doing "what you could"
for the war effort. So "one day, instead of going to work I
joined the Navy," she said. "They called my boss and he gave
me a terrific reference, you know, and so they took me on
the spot although I was awfully shocked. . . . I'm just barely
five feet you know. The doctor said, 'Somebody lied for
you!'" The services were desperate to fill their ranks with
qualified people and were not about to let her get away
because she lacked a half inch in height!

The mobilization was like nothing ever seen before in
U.S. history. As Powers recalled:

Women who want to enlist in the Navy wait at a Marine recruiting station.

In those days, just before the war there were beggars ... walking the street, and they went in people's houses, and they asked for something to eat. And my mother always, always gave them something hot and a sandwich.... But the thing was the war came and there were no more beggars.... If they didn't have a home all they had to do was join the Army or the Navy. No more beggars after the war. Everybody could get work, it didn't make any difference what condition you were. Men were so scarce, women who hadn't worked in years and years went in the factories.[5]

As military mobilization continued, the United States was quickly transformed into a global force. Troops prepared to go "over there," the term most Americans used to refer to the battlefields abroad.

Three

★

OVER THERE

Most U.S. soldiers did not immediately go to the war zone. Instead, they were sent into rigorous training. John Joseph "Black Jack" Pershing was the general of the army in charge of the American Expeditionary Force, and he would not allow his men to go into combat before they were adequately trained. He insisted that U.S. soldiers become excellent marksmen and seasoned troops before they faced the enemy.

He did not want his troops to serve as replacements for the weary, war-ravaged soldiers who were confined to the murderous trenches in Europe. Instead, he planned to break the trench warfare that had been grinding down the British and French armies for two years. General Pershing held steady to his plan, but often it seemed that he would have to fight the Allies, too, as he insisted that his army be allowed to operate independently.

While the training and bickering about the manner in which the U.S. forces would serve went on, the war did not take a holiday. The Central Powers and the Allies fought each other on many fronts across Europe, in Italy and other parts of the Mediterranean, and in battles waged over German colonies in Africa, Asia, and the Pacific Islands.

The African campaigns were especially brutal, but they

U.S. troops in training

were regarded as mere sideshows and were largely ignored in Europe and the United States, even though many thousands of Europeans, Arabs, Indians, and Africans took part. Battles raged "over tens of thousands of square miles, much of it unmapped and unexplored" and were fought "by tattered, hungry men in dust and mud, rain and broiling heat," according to Byron Farwell, author of numerous war books. Farwell explained one reason little is known about this aspect of the Great War: "Most of those involved were illiterate; few of the literate participants recorded their experiences, and historians were not present. Records were badly kept, for few of the fighting units were regular regiments, and climatic conditions contributed to the destruction of many that were kept."[1]

OBSERVATIONS FROM THE FRONT LINE

In contrast to Allied campaigns against the Germans on other continents, Allied battles against the Central Powers in Europe were regularly recorded. Even before Americans began preparations for fighting in Europe, reporters, photographers, and others from the United States had been documenting the battles. Observers sent home reports that were often used to build support in the United States for the war abroad.

Robert McCormick, an Illinois National Guardsman, was at the Russian front in 1915. He wrote down his observations for the folks back home as he and a filmmaker visited the scene of battle. Once, in the trenches, he was allowed to peer through a periscope that was pointed toward the enemy line:

> By focusing a field glass into the periscope I detect about fifty yards away the wire entanglements of the German army, and behind that a line in the earth where lies the firing trench.
>
> Crack—bluck!
>
> I have been too deliberate. A good glass has detected the periscope and a sharpshooter has hoped to find a weak spot where the officer's head is revealed.

McCormick reported that the photographer had the camera up and "grinding away at a real battle scene. The Germans are fighting fast, the crack of their rifles, the buck of the bullets in the parapet, and the strange crack-whistle of those flying overhead being continuous."

Although McCormick wanted photographs of "the smoke puffs across the way," that would have meant "certain death." So the photographer took pictures of the bullet-riddled trees to prove that the two men had been at the front. Then, as they made their way toward safety, they were stopped by a friendly Russian orderly. As McCormick reported:

> The regimental volunteer meets us, a twelve-year-old typical kind. His face is wet with honest sweat, from carrying our presents, two empty shrapnel cases and fuses. He is freckled and sunburnt. He has a speech to make, but has forgotten it. And there is not an American boy alive who does not envy him.[2]

Another war correspondent, Richard Harding Davis, along with reporter James Hare, visited the French and British forces in France and Salonika, Greece. In the fall of 1915, Allied troops had been sent to Salonika in an attempt to set up positions to defend Serbia.

Davis described his trip into the mountainous Balkan region as "desolate and bleak," with rain and snow running down the hillsides and turning "the land into a sea of mud." He saw soldiers all along the way fighting the mud, shoveling it off roadways and trying to wash it from their clothes and bodies in icy water from a lake.

When Davis and Hare reached the front line, they came upon a small British battery ready to go into action. "The men behind the guns were extremely young, but like most artillerymen, alert, sinewy, springing to their appointed tasks with swift, catlike certainty. . . . There were two boy officers in command, one certainly not yet eighteen, his superior officer still under twenty," Davis reported.

Although the young soldiers tried to appear menacing, they quickly welcomed the strangers, and Davis reported that he "felt like taking one of the boy officers under each arm, and smuggling him safely home to his mother." Davis asked if the young soldiers had any support, and one of the officers "gazed around him. It was growing dark and gloomier, and the hollows of the white hills were filled with shadows. His men were listening, so he said bravely, with a vague sweep of the hand at the encircling darkness, 'Oh, they're about—somewhere,' adding that his station might be called an independent command."

As Davis prepared to leave the battery position, he gave one officer some cigars known as King of England cigars, apologizing because they were not made in England and were of poor quality. But the officer gladly accepted the gifts, saying he would smoke them even if they "were called the 'German Emperor.'"

Davis left feeling that he had deserted the small squad and that "the mother of each [soldier] could hold me to account" for her son's life. "As we drove away . . . I could see in the twilight the flashes of the guns and two lonely specks of light. They were the 'King of England' cigars burning bravely."[3]

Not long after this encounter, English and French troops were forced to retreat as more powerful Austrian armies closed in. Along with the French and English, some remnants of the Serbian army plus thousands of refugees fled toward the Adriatic Sea and safety in Allied territory.

FIGHTING IN THE TRENCHES

As the war ground on, the fighting forces in the trenches faced a bizarre existence. Soldiers were rotated in and out of the front lines, sometimes going to the countryside, where they bathed, rested, ate well, and drank the low-priced wines available. Then, back in the trenches, they were faced with the misery of mud, slugs, frogs, rodents, lice, and often utter boredom.

Charles Edmonds, a young soldier in the British

Digging trenches in France in March 1918

Expeditionary Force, described in his memoirs the world
that was created in the trenches to defend French soil:

> By day there was really not much to do. Sometimes working
> parties could be organised, if the trench to be dug or
> drained was passable by daylight. A memorable day it was
> when two of us had drained a long communication trench
> called Fifth Avenue, penning the mud and water behind a
> temporary dam of clay, in a dead end—a grand game of mud
> pies for a boy on a spring morning. Then came the news
> that the brigadier and his staff were coming up the trench.

Now trenches wind in curious zigzags lest enemy guns should be able to rake them, shooting along them in a straight line from end to end. The brigadier, though only a few yards away, could see and know nothing of our doings round the corner. We broke down the dam, releasing a flood of liquid slime, knee deep, glutinous, stinking, which swept him away. No gilded staff officers appeared after that to interrupt our innocent ease in the front line.

In a more serious manner, Edmonds explained that the troops on both sides of no man's land—the expanse of land between them—waited until dark before most major activities began. Then soldiers dug more trenches and strung more wire "in pitchy blackness." He wrote:

Heavy labour ... in awkward places must be relentlessly performed without showing a light or making a sound. Some skilled officers and men crawled, boy-scout fashion, to listen and observe near the enemy's lines ... through the darkness, peering over the parapet into the open field (the Racecourse, they called it) bounded two hundred yards away by the German wire entanglement, behind which in equal darkness and silence the unseen, unheard enemy watched and sweated and laboured in just the same way.[4]

Leslie Buswell was a volunteer from the United States who drove an ambulance to the battlefields where the French and British were fighting. His job, in many cases, was to help bury the dead. "It sounds very simple, doesn't it?" he wrote in one letter home to his family. "Do you realize what it means? It means handling terrible objects covered with blood-soaked clothing, that once had the shape of human beings. It means taking from these forms all articles of apparel that might prove serviceable and searching through these red-stained clothes for any letters or identification. Some of these shapes are stiff and cold. Some are mere fragments."[5]

In another letter, he described a situation that his French friends in the trenches near Soissons had to endure: "When the trenches are very close to each other, a little advance post is dug so that one can hear what is being said by the enemy in their trenches. Generally, however, the distance between the lines is too great for this, and at night a soldier is sent out to crawl within hearing distance of the enemy." During one such mission, a soldier was hit by enemy fire and

when daylight came he was seen to be struggling to crawl back to his friends. Two soldiers promptly started out to help him, but on reaching him the Germans shot and wounded them, so that the three men were now crying to their comrades to come and save them.

... As soon as darkness fell, two other soldiers crept forth, but no sooner had they reached the three wounded than an illuminating rocket disclosed their positions to the enemy, and left five men lying wounded between the lines. As the captain could not afford to lose his men in this futile way, he detailed two sentries to shoot any one attempting to leave. The five men lay there shouting to their friends— calling them by their names—reminding them of their friendship—and asking if they were going to allow their comrades to die thus without help.

Finally, two members of the Red Cross came into the trench and discovered the soldiers in a terrible state of anxiety over their inability to protect their friends. Since the Red Cross was not under military control, "they promptly left the trench to save the five wounded Frenchmen—*Seven* men are still there between friend and foe,—but at peace now, God willing."[6]

Peace was not to come for the remainder of the combatants until the American Expeditionary Force took up positions on the lines of battle. Even though the French and British were dedicated fighters who were willing to sacrifice everything to defend their lands and people, they and the other Allies knew a major German offensive would probably be successful. It was obvious the Allies needed help. Ready or not, General Pershing ordered his troops to Europe.

Four

✦

ACROSS THE ATLANTIC

As we turned a corner and looked ahead, there lay the
ocean and a trim troopship riding proudly at the wharf....
This was it!....When all the freight, equipment, troops and
ammunition would be loaded, we would cast off.... About 7
o'clock, darkness settled over the harbor. Soon there came
to our ears the shrill commanding tones of tug boat whis-
tles....

Orders were given that everyone aboard should go
below, and remain there out of sight until further notice. At
length the great troopship was silently moving out to sea.
After a few hours of discomfort, all those who desired were
given permission to go out on the decks.... Far away to the
southwest a glimmer of light grew fainter as the ship bore
on. We were leaving the only things we knew and loved.[1]

That was the recollection of new army recruit Stuart
Robson as he left Hoboken, New Jersey, in January of 1918
with thousands of other soldiers of the American
Expeditionary Force. They were on their way across the
Atlantic Ocean to France and the war. Some two million
Americans made this passage, half of them on Allied ships.
The other half sailed on captured German vessels or on refit-
ted merchant transports, as was the case with Stuart Robson's

*Troop transport ships were protected by convoys
to lessen the possibility of attack by German U-boats.*

voyage. As he explained, "The ship bears the name *Great Northern,* and it is said to have plied between California and Hawaii as a passenger and fruit boat before being converted into a troop transport."[2]

U-BOATS AND MINES

The German plan to terrorize the high seas with surprise U-boat attacks had been blunted by the American and English practice of providing protective convoys for ships making the dangerous passage in the Atlantic or the North Sea. The countermeasure was generally successful. In fact, no troops traveling to Europe on any of the converted transports were lost at sea.

Not everyone was safe from attack, however. The submarines were still capable of causing much destruction, as Stuart Robson learned from some men on his ship who told how a torpedo had sunk "a ship called the *Tuscania* . . . a British ship carrying American soldiers to France. . . . After two days in the cold waters of the North Atlantic, the survivors . . . had been rescued and brought ashore on the coast of Scotland."[3]

Norbert Hayden was part of a crew on a ship that carried soldiers like Robson out of Hoboken to Brest or Calais, France. Hayden was assigned to a converted troop transport called the USS *George Washington*, and he described the precautions taken on board the ship to protect against enemy weapons:

> It was all camouflaged on the outside, it looked like lightning. Black and white stripes [were painted] on it to ward off submarines. They said they can't see the ship as well when that's on there.
>
> I made ten round trips to France from New York. When you got to the English Channel it was always rough. We were always on the lookout for submarines and mines. They had mines all over the place. Mines were anchored to a cable below the surface, and our mine sweepers would cut that cable and the mine would come to the top and men would shoot it to explode it. And I heard them a lot of times dropping depth bombs. Whenever they saw a submarine they would drop them. And then we would have to get away fast because of the concussion. No matter how far

away we got from the explosion, when the concussion hit the side of our boat, it sounded like a steel hammer hit it. It was always a danger.[4]

German U-boat attacks and exploding mines were not the only concerns. The natural danger of sea travel made the almost two-week trip across the ocean quite adventurous. In Hayden's words:

The first night out at New York all the lights were off on the ship. They don't have no headlights or nothing on them ships at night. Only on the inside and all the doors are closed. I slept in a hammock that night, and every night. The first night I was okay, slept good on the hammock, but just as soon as my feet hit that deck in the morning I was seasick. I had to go to the topside bad, quick. I survived. I never got so sick that I couldn't do my work. I was waiting on tables, mess cook, and all kind of things like that, and I never had to go to the sick bay.

One time we had such a bad storm. This time we were taking President Woodrow Wilson over there. When the president was on, we always had a convoy: all kinds of battle-ships circling around us. When we went into the storm, the other ships couldn't take it, and they had to go to the Azores [islands in the North Atlantic], and we had to stay out there and fight that storm. The wooden life boats up on top were all broke-in, just like kindling, from the waves hitting over the top.[5]

AT THE FRONT

Once their journey across the Atlantic was completed, U.S. soldiers landed in France. Robson arrived at the French port of Brest, and reported that

Colored soldiers dressed in old-fashioned blue uniforms like that of the Spanish-American War were doing steve-dore work on the docks around the ships which fly our flag. These were American soldiers and they shouted greetings to us as we crowded the rail of the *Great Northern*. . . . Rumor had it that we would ride a French railroad train to the front.[6]

When the Americans landed in France, the German command was gambling that an all-out offensive against the enemy would finally lead to a victory for the Central Powers, if it could be accomplished before the inexperienced Yanks were fully ready to fight. But the Americans launched their first attack in late May 1918 at Cantigny, northwest of the Marne River, and won a major battle against veteran German troops. This victory proved to be a real boost for the Allies, convincing them that they could turn the tide in their favor.

At the same time, U.S. forces were moving into position along the Marne. With the French, they were able to hold the bridges at Château-Thierry and drive the Germans back across the river. West of the city of Reims, fourteen German divisions crossed the Marne again, but Americans halted the advance. Then Allied aircraft and artillery bombed bridges and wrecked supply lines, making certain that the Germans would be forced to retreat.

On August 30, Pershing ordered his troops toward St.-Mihiel, a frontline area that had been occupied by the enemy since the beginning of the war in 1914. About 1,400 planes of the Allied Air Force, under the command of U.S. Colonel Billy Mitchell, provided protective cover for troops on the ground, and the U.S. First Army attacked from two directions. Once more the American plan was successful, and the area was cleared of enemy troops.

Allied forces halted the German advance at the Marne River in France.

BLACK TROOPS WITH FRENCH FORCES

Some of the U.S. troops sent to Europe were assigned to units fighting with the French under the command of the newly appointed supreme commander of the Allied forces, French general Ferdinand Foch. As Pershing prepared to send U.S. soldiers abroad, he also sent a warning to French military leaders about the status of black troops. In a secret memorandum, Pershing warned the French not to share meals with blacks or to be too friendly or to commend them. Pershing believed such behavior would offend white soldiers. In short, he expected the French to treat black soldiers as they were treated in the United States—like second-class citizens or worse.[7]

Such discrimination was not as commonplace in Europe as it was in the United States, but the Germans tried to exploit American racism. Germans distributed propaganda leaflets among African-American soldiers stating that blacks were sent to Europe to make the world safe for democracy even though they had few rights in their own land.

Nevertheless, many blacks believed they should be loyal to their country and they served with distinction. The most successful black regiments served under the French command and were cited for bravery by the French, although their feats were seldom acknowledged by the U.S. Army.

Clifton Merriman, an African-American enlistee from Cambridge, Massachusetts, became part of a regiment sent to France. Merriman, who was promoted to staff sergeant in early 1918, led his all-black platoon against a large German machine gun nest that had been inflicting heavy losses on his men. Using hand grenades, the platoon killed the gunner and others in the trenches. Interviewed when he was eighty-nine years old, Merriman recalled:

I then led what remained of my platoon to positions and held the nest until we were reinforced early the next morning. During the engagement, my gas mask was riddled with bullets from machine gun attacks and I was without protection from repeated gas attacks. I was severely gassed, and was evacuated to a first aid station behind the lines. After treatment I returned to the front lines.[8]

Sergeant Clifton Merriman of the all-black 372nd Infantry Regiment received the Croix de Guerre from France. This medal was awarded for gallantry in war.

When Merriman returned to the United States, the Commonwealth of Massachusetts recognized him for his bravery. But it was not until years later, in 1982, that the Army National Guard finally presented Merriman and nine other black men citations for their patriotic services in World War I.

No black soldier in World War I received the highest U.S. military decoration, the Medal of Honor, until 1993, when the U.S. Army followed up on recommendations to honor black servicemen. President George Bush presented a posthumous Medal of Honor to the family of Corporal Freddie Stowers, who had died many years before. In presenting the award for "conspicuous gallantry" and risking "life above and beyond the call of duty," Bush described how Stowers led an all-black company against the Germans:

> Only a few minutes after the fighting began, the enemy stopped firing and enemy troops climbed out of their trenches onto the parapets of the trench, held up their arms

and seemed to surrender. The relieved American forces held their fire, stepped out into the open. As our troops moved forward, the enemy jumped back into their trenches and sprayed our men with ... machine-gun and mortar fire. The assault annihilated more than 50 percent of Company C. And in the midst of this bloody chaos, Corporal Stowers took charge and bravely led his men forward, destroying the foes.[9]

Stowers was wounded, but he urged his men forward. He died during the attack and was buried in Meuse-Argonne American Cemetery in France.

Five

★

AIR POWER

During World War I, new "aeroplanes," as they were called, were developed, providing a great advantage as weaponry used in dropping bombs and firing machine guns. Such planes as Sopwith Camels and Fokkers became well known as fighter aircraft.

The skilled and daring pilots who flew these planes were the first ever to do combat in the sky and added a new battleground to military conflict. The flimsy planes were made of canvas and wood. Pilots sat in open cockpits, usually flying with another aviator who was an observer and gunner. Aviators wore goggles and helmets, which they usually had to buy themselves. When they flew at high altitudes, they put on oxygen masks and electrically heated suits as protection against the cold, thin air. It was not unusual for aviators flying in extreme cold to suffer frostbite.

GETTING INTO THE AIR

When the United States declared war on Germany, the U.S. Navy and Marine Corps combined had only fifty-four airplanes and less than 300 aviators. The navy immediately recruited more than one hundred men and sent them to France for training as the First Aeronautical Detachment,

Brigadier General Billy Mitchell was air adviser
to General Pershing. Mitchell commanded several
air units in combat during World War I.

America's first organized military unit to arrive in the combat zone. Using French and British aircraft, enlistees learned about aviation and air warfare in the midst of the fighting.

Even before the U.S. involvement, American pilots had gone to France to help bolster the French government's air force. One of those pilots was James McConnell, who was with the American Escadrille, a flying corps stationed at Verdun in 1915. In an account of his experiences, he described how his squadron prepared to take off for battle. A pilot waited for a mechanic to shriek "Contact!" and then

> Contact! you reply. You snap on the switch, he spins the propeller, and the motor takes. Drawing forward out of line, you put on full power, race across the grass and take air. . . . In three minutes you are at about 4,000 feet. You have been

making wide circles over the field and watching the other machines. At 4,500 feet you throttle down and wait for your companions to catch up. Soon the escadrille is bunched and off for the lines.[1]

During battle, pilots often flew their planes so close to one another that they could see facial expressions or "the death jerk of [a pilot's] helmeted head as bullets struck between the shoulders," according to one British pilot, Arthur Gould Lee, who was with the Royal Flying Corps. Lee noted in a foreword to a collection of his war letters that air combat was at times

tinged with something of the knightly chivalry of old, when a pilot, perhaps still in his teens, might inwardly salute his antagonist, even wave to him as they circled each other, seeking the chance to fire. And having killed, could feel pity for a fellow flyer ... could even respect and admire ... skill and valour. Yet ... every man fought with but one purpose—to kill or be killed.[2]

Besides the obvious dangers of combat, there were other flight hazards. In many instances, engines failed and planes plunged to the ground or into the sea, killing aviators instantly. If they survived after a crash, their calls for help often had to be sent by carrier pigeon. "We carry four pigeons for messengers in case of motor trouble or accidents of any kind," explained Irving Sheely, an enlisted officer and observer-gunner with the U.S. Navy's First Aeronautical Detachment. While stationed in France, Sheely reported in a letter home that his squadron once received an urgent message for help from "these little messengers," and responded with a rescue crew to pull a survivor from a "flying boat" (seaplane) that had crashed into the North Sea.[3]

While pilots were training or in combat, it was not unusual for them to occasionally fall from their cockpits. Sheely witnessed two such incidents; in one, the pilot was killed, but in the other, "an army man was thrown out but he landed on the tail of his machine and crawled back in. . . . The poor fellow was somewhat frightened, but he didn't lose his nerve."[4]

One of the tactics of air warfare was the dogfight, which McConnell with the American Escadrille described:

> Getting started is the hardest part of an attack. Once you have begun diving you're all right. The pilot just ahead turns tail up like a trout dropping back to water, and swoops down in irregular curves and circles. You follow at an angle so steep your feet seem to be holding you back in your seat. Now the black Maltese crosses on the German's wings stand out clearly. You think of him as some sort of big bug. Then you hear the rapid tut-tut-tut of his machine gun. . . .
>
> The rattle of the gun that is aimed at you leaves you undisturbed. Only when the bullets pierce the wings a few feet from off do you become uncomfortable. You see the gunner crouched down behind his weapon, but you aim at where the pilot ought to be—there are two men aboard the German craft—and press on the release hard. . . . Then, hopefully, you look back at the foe. He ought to be dropping earthward at several miles a minute. As a matter of fact, however, he is sailing serenely on. They have an annoying habit of doing that.[5]

THE GERMAN ACE

One German pilot who always seemed to escape Allied aircraft was Manfred Freiherr von Richthofen, nicknamed the Red Baron because he flew a red Fokker triplane. The Red

A dogfight between British and German airplanes

Baron became the most feared pilot of World War I. (Years later, his feats were the inspiration for the character Snoopy in the comic strip "Peanuts.")

Richthofen joined the military well before there was any German air force. "I entered the Cadet Corps as a boy of eleven," he wrote. "I was not particularly eager to become a cadet, but my father wished it, and I was not consulted."[6]

After graduating, Richthofen moved along in his career to the cavalry, where he became an officer at the age of twenty. Two years later, the war began, and he was assigned to the Russian front. By 1916, he was trained to fly, and by early

1918, he was credited with shooting down eighty Allied planes. But on April 21, 1918, he crossed the path of Captain Roy Brown, a Canadian flying with the British Royal Flying Corps, which was returning from a mission. As Captain Brown remembered that day:

> On the way home we met a number of enemy fliers. We got into a fight, and I want to say at the outset that after a few seconds I had given up hope of ever coming out of this engagement alive. I looked over at my friend Captain May [in another plane], and my heart beat with joy despite all the trouble, as I saw that May had succeeded in shooting down a German flier. May immediately turned from his victory to fly home.... But the moment he flew off, I saw a red airplane set out after him.... As I went to help him, I had to fight for my own life, as three fliers came down to crush me. I was in a crossfire of their guns, with no way out! In any event, I wanted to make it as unpleasant as possible for them!

Through a series of daring maneuvers including spirals, dives, and back loops, Brown was finally able to lose the three Germans. Safe from immediate attack by his pursuers, he turned his thoughts once more to his friend. He spotted May flying in the direction of home:

> He was still being followed. From out of the mist a bright red airplane shot after him in such an advantageous position as to be easily fatal for him. I climbed further up to eventually bring help to May. He tried to get away...zigzagging, but the "red one" stayed steadfastly behind him.... Suddenly it became clear that May was in a trap.

Captain Brown was now at 3,000 feet (900 meters) and in a position to finally aid his friend, who seemed to have given up and was "ready for the death blow," as Brown put it. But Brown was able to attack the "red one":

> I dove down until I was on his tail, then I fired. The bullets tore into his elevator and mutilated the rear part of the airplane. Flames showed where the bullets struck.
>
> Aimed too short! Quite gradually I pulled on the stick.... I came up a little, it was like gunnery-school practice. A full burst ripped into the side of the airplane. The pilot turned around and looked back. I saw the glint of his eyes behind the big goggles, then he collapsed in the seat, bullets whistled by him. I ceased firing.
>
> Richthofen was dead. It all happened in seconds, faster than one can tell. His airplane shook, tottered, rolled over and plunged down.[7]

REACHING AN ARMISTICE

*T*he air war was certainly the most romantic arena of this very bloody conflict, and stories of the pilots' daring exploits made good reading in Europe and the United States. While the planes afforded some advantage to the troops on the ground, the final victory was achieved because ordinary men and women sacrificed their comfort, their dreams, and too often their lives by doing the dirty day-to-day tasks that war requires.

Because so many men served in the military—more than at any other time in history—life for those who were left behind was anything but normal. The contributions made by nonmilitary folks at home and near the front were crucial to the war effort. Rationing of common goods, foods, and services was the law throughout Europe as all matériel was diverted to the weapons factories or to the front.

Early in the war, there were constant efforts in Europe (and later in the United States after the draft was instituted) to recruit for the military through newspaper notices, articles, and posters. One British notice spoke "To the Young Women of London" and asked: "Is your 'Best Boy' wearing Khaki? If not don't *YOU THINK* he should be? If he does not think that you and your country are worth fighting for—do you think he is *WORTHY* of you?"[1]

In the United States, there were calls for volunteers to donate blood and for citizens to conserve on wheat, meat, sugar, and fats so that these staples could be sent to the army. Americans collected books to send "over there" to the armed forces and heeded the American Red Cross slogan to "do your bit—save the pit." People saved fruit pits and seeds, which were used to produce carbon for gas masks. Citizens also bought U.S. government bonds and war stamps to support Liberty Loans. Almost $10 billion in U.S. loans went to the Allies to help pay for weapons and other military equipment, while about $23 billion was spent for the U.S. war effort.

Girl Scouts collected peach pits to aid the war effort.
The pits were used to produce carbon for gas masks.

Prior to the war, women were truly second-class citizens in most parts of the world. They often did not have the right to vote, they rarely worked outside the home, and their lives were generally regarded as secondary to those of their husbands and children. As the nineteenth century came to a close, women in England and the United States began to organize and demand more political and social power. Men wanted to maintain the status quo and their dominance, so they fought against the feminist ideas that were discussed. Certainly, they would argue, women can't do the work of men! Their place is in the home, being cared for by a protective husband, they declared.

The war put aside those arguments, since there were not enough men around to provide a protective arm or to take care of basic needs. Without men to do their regular work in the mills, the farms, or the offices, women had to pick up the slack.

Helen Fraser reported in 1918 on women's service to England, noting that "the women of all the allies are one in this great struggle. . . . Our work is the same task of supporting and sustaining the energies of our men in arms and our nations at home." She noted that from the beginning, women "volunteered in tens of thousands, every kind of woman, young, old, middle-aged, rich and poor, trained and untrained." At the time, there were "1,250,000 women in industry directly replacing men, 1,000,000 in munitions, 83,000 additional women in Government Departments," plus another 258,300 women working outside the home full- or part-time. Other women were recruited "for the Women's Army Auxiliary Corps at the rate of 10,000 a month." A Women's Royal Naval Service was initiated, and about 60,000 women served with the Red Cross "in hospitals in England

This woman is part of the work force in a munitions factory.

and France, and our other fronts, in addition to our thousands of trained nurses."[2]

Food was in short supply, and producing more for an ever-increasing army was an almost impossible challenge. "Within nine months of the outbreak of war, it was clear we must secure help for the farmers," wrote Fraser. "As the submarine menace developed, and the supply of grain in the world was affected by the numbers of men taken away from production," a means had to be found to grow more food. To convince farmers that they should accept women who were members of the Women's Land Army as farmhands, "exhibitions of farm work were arranged in different part[s] of the country with great success, and the girls showed they could plough, and weed and hoe and milk and care for stock, and do all the farm work, except the heaviest, extremely well."

Fraser explained that as a result of these demonstrations, "the farmer who used to declare he would never have a woman and that they were no use, and who has them now, is always quite pleased and generally cherishes a profound conviction that the reason why his women are all right is because he has the most exceptional ones in the country."[3]

*These members of the Women's Land Army in England
are shown using a steam plow to turn the land.*

Addie Hunton and Kathryn Johnson were two African-American women—volunteers from the United States—who were assigned work much closer to the action in Europe. They served as secretaries for the YMCA (Young Men's Christian Association), one of several service organizations that set up social clubs for the men on the line. As the armed services were still segregated at that time, Hunton and Johnson were among the very few women administering to the emotional needs of the men of color in France. They reported having contact

with a hundred thousand men, many of whom it was our privilege to help in a hundred different ways; men who were groping and discouraged; others who were crying loudly for help, that they might acquire just the rudiments of an education, and so establish connection with the anxious hearts whom they had left behind; and still others who had a depth of understanding and a breadth of vision that was at once a help and an inspiration.[4]

The armed services in World War I were segregated and so were the social clubs set up for servicemen.

WINNING ON THE BATTLEFRONT

Civilian efforts and technological advances such as those made in airplanes were important to the war effort, but it was the men of the infantry who finally turned the tide and crushed the German will to continue the war. After the success of the American soldiers at the St.-Mihiel battlefront, Pershing was faced with the difficult task of moving his force of almost one million to a new battle line 60 miles (100 kilometers) away.

During the night, so as not to attract the attention of German spotter planes, the American Expeditionary Force marched and drove its tanks and guns to the Argonne Forest, west of the Meuse River. Here General Foch, commander of all the Allied armies, was ready to launch the final major offensive. The British would strike one section of the German lines, and a French-American attack was to start at Verdun and move to Mezieres in the Meuse Valley, where the goal was to cut enemy railroad supply lines.

The assault began in late September 1918. Initially, the Americans made good headway, but the Germans brought up reinforcements at the Argonne Forest, where an October battle made Sergeant Alvin C. York the most familiar name of World War I.

York was the most unlikely young man to be a hero of any war. Raised in the mountains of Tennessee, York had strong religious convictions against killing and declared himself a conscientious objector. But in time, and after much prayer, this simple mountaineer decided that it was necessary to join the fight.

York wound up leading a small squad of men in an attack on a German machine gun nest in the Argonne, killing twenty-five of the enemy and winning that position. Then York, virtually alone, captured another 132 German soldiers. For his actions, he was awarded the Medal of Honor and more than fifty other decorations.

His recollection of the men who fought with him in Europe provides some insight on how the war was finally won. To him, it was not too complicated, and like his shooting, his views were right on target:

> Over here in the training camps and behind the lines in France a right-smart lot of them boozed, gambled, cussed, and went A.W.O.L. But once they got into it Over There they kept on a-going. They were only tol'able shots and burned up a most awful lot of ammunition. But jest the same they always kept a-going. Most of them died like men, with their rifles and bayonets in their hands and their faces to the enemy. I'm a-thinkin' they were real heroes.[5]

CALLS FOR PEACE

The victory at the Argonne and the push by the Americans and French that finally cut through the third German line of defense were a death blow for the enemy cause. By the end of October, the German government was asking President Wilson to negotiate a peace.

The president had written a proposal for peace based on Fourteen Points. These points set down a vision for a new world with fair treatment of all nations and the establishment of a League of Nations, where countries' representatives could meet to discuss cooperative efforts and to solve conflicts. Wilson said that "peace should rest upon the rights of peoples, not the rights of governments—the rights of peoples, great or small . . . to freedom and security and self-government and to . . . economic opportunities."[6]

An armistice was eventually signed in a ceremony that took place on the eleventh hour of the eleventh day of the

When Germany surrendered, the armistice was signed in train car No. 2419D (foreground). Years later, when France surrendered to Germany during World War II, Hitler chose the same train car for the signing of the armistice.

eleventh month of 1918, a long four and a half years after the start of the conflict that was to be the "war to end all wars." But the peace treaty that was eventually worked out bore little resemblance to the humanitarian dream that President Wilson had outlined in his Fourteen Points. The Allied nations made secret deals for territory and demanded compensation from the defeated Germans, Austrians, and Turks. As a result, the boundaries of Europe were redrawn and the League of Nations experiment was doomed, killing chances for a future of cooperation.

As a World War I veteran, Herbert Engleman, said on the seventy-fifth anniversary of the signing of the armistice: "The world only got worse, I guess, and got a lot dumber. We just don't learn from our experiences. War never will end. And it will never solve a thing."[7]

Source Notes

One

1. Quoted in Norm Maves, Jr., "Old Soldiers Take a Dim View of War," *Oregonian*, November 11, 1993, E8.

2. Quoted in Elizabeth Mullener, "Vet, 95, Recalls Joyful End to War," *New Orleans Times Picayune*, November 11, 1993, A1.

3. Quoted in John M. Blum et al., *The National Experience*, 2nd ed. (New York: Harcourt, Brace and World, 1968), 596.

4. Ibid.

5. *"Mademoiselle Miss"; letters from an American girl serving with the rank of lieutenant in a French army hospital at the front* (Boston: W. A. Butterfield, 1916), 21–23.

Two

1. Quoted in Blum et al., *National Experience*, 589.

2. Quoted in Candace Serena Falk, *Love, Anarchy, and Emma Goldman* (New York: Holt, Rinehart and Winston, 1984; reprint, New Brunswick, N.J.: Rutgers University Press, 1990), 156.

3. Norbert Ephraim Hayden, interview by Dean Hamilton, tape recording, December 12, 1993, Tampa, Fla.

4. Ibid.

5. Claire Lyon Powers, interview by Dean Hamilton, tape recording, December 12, 1993, Tampa, Fla.

Three

1. Byron Farwell, *The Great War in Africa, 1914–1918* (New York: W. W. Norton, 1986), 14–15.

2. Robert R. McCormick, *With the Russian Army* (New York: Macmillan Company, 1915), 94–96.

3. Richard Harding Davis, *With the French in France and Salonika* (New York: Charles Scribners Sons, 1916), 152–164.

4. Charles Edmonds, *A Subaltern's War* (London: Peter Davies, 1929), 22–24.

5. Leslie Buswell, *Ambulance no. 10, personal letters from the front* (Boston: Houghton Mifflin, 1916), 133.

6. Ibid., 137–139.

Four

1. Stuart Robson, *It's Old Stuff Now* (New York: Vantage Press, 1976), 3.

2. Ibid., 5.

3. Ibid., 24–25.

4. Hayden, interview.

5. Ibid.

6. Robson, *It's Old Stuff Now*, 12–13.

7. Robert W. Mullen, *Blacks in America's Wars*, 8th ed. (New York: Pathfinder, 1991), 44.

8. Quoted in William R. Cash, "Senior Set War Hero Recalls the Fury of Battle," *Boston Globe*, December 5, 1982, Living section, 1.

9. Quoted in Donnie Radcliffe, "Black Soldier Gets Recognition 73 Years Late," *Oregonian*, April 26, 1991, A14.

Five

1. James R. McConnell, *Flying for France* (Garden City, N.Y.: Doubleday, Page and Company, 1917), 50.

2. Arthur Gould Lee, *No Parachute: A Fighter Pilot in World War I* (London: Jarrolds Publishers, 1968), xv–xvi.

3. Laurence D. Sheely, ed., *Sailor of the Air* (Tuscaloosa, Ala.: University of Alabama Press, 1993), 123–124.

4. Ibid., 151–152.

5. McConnell, *Flying for France*, 59–61.

6. Quoted in Stanley M. Ulanoff, ed., *The Red Baron* (Garden City, N.Y.: Doubleday and Company, 1969), 1.

7. Ibid., 143–145.

Six

1. From a poster reproduced in Maurice Rickards, *Posters of the First World War* (New York: Walker and Company, 1968), 23.

2. Helen Fraser, *Women and War Work* (New York: C. Arnold Shaw, 1918), 20–21.

3. Ibid., 163–164.

4. Addie W. Hunton and Kathryn M. Johnson, *Two Colored Women with the American Expeditionary Forces* (Brooklyn, N.Y.: Brooklyn Eagle Press, [1920?]), 22.

5. Quoted in Tom Skeyhill, ed., epigraph to *Sergeant York: His Own Life Story and War Diary* (Garden City, N.Y.: Doubleday, Doran and Company, 1930).

6. Quoted in Blum et al., *National Experience*, 602.

7. Quoted in Maves, "Old Soldiers," E8.

Further Reading

Brown, Gene. *Conflict in Europe and the Great Depression: World War I.* New York: Twenty-First Century Books, 1993.

Kent, Zachary. *World War I: "The War to End Wars."* Hillside, N.J.: Enslow, 1994.

Roth-Hano, Renee. *Touch Wood: A Girlhood in Occupied France.* New York: Puffin, 1989.

Sanford, Bill, and Carl Green. *The World War I Soldier at Chateau Thierry.* Mankato, Minn.: Capstone, 1991.

Stewart, Gail. *World War One.* San Diego: Lucent, 1991.

Index